PARATOM'S

GUIDE TO PARANORMAL INVESTIGATIONS

Thomas Lynch

Julie Williams

Copyright © 2011 Thomas Lynch, Julie Williams

www.ParaTom.com

ISBN: 13:978-1456466954

CONTENTS

On the set of "Spektral Evidence"   A HCTV Production   (2010)

ACKNOWLEDGMENTS

For thousands of years, man has longed to know what is beyond the thin veil that separates the living from the dead. I am also one of those looking to unravel this mystery. I cannot do it alone. I depend on a system of supports. For one, I would like to thank my manager and contributing author, *Julie Williams*, for helping out with the mundane tasks of getting our name out there, setting up the gazillion appointments that just seem to happen randomly, and being the go-between for the client and myself. Thank you Julie for all the work you are doing for ParaTom.com.

Secondly, I would like to acknowledge the efforts of all the investigators working to bring some relevance and legitimacy to this field. You know who you are. To you, I say "thank you".

Finally, I would like to acknowledge those that I have handpicked to work directly with me as I need them, past and present. They give up their time without asking for anything in return. They are level headed individuals that come to an investigation ready to be professional, courteous and attentive to the client. *Lori Hand, Phil Lynch* and on occasion, *Deb O'Leary, (of Pelham Paranormal)* thank you for being the type of people that I am proud to bring along on an investigation.

I need to say early in this book that the field of paranormal investigation and research is a pseudo science, and is not accepted as a true science. That is because evidence cannot be recreated in a controlled environment. With that said have fun and try to make a difference in the field.

"I dedicate this book to my dad, the late *Neil F. Lynch*, who is with me, always, in spirit. And my kids, *Jonathan* and *Amanda*, who I cannot get to believe in anything paranormal, but who continue to believe in me."

Section One
SETTING UP YOUR INVESTIGATIVE UNIT

When I was younger, I would venture into local cemeteries and just sit. I loved being in these colonial cemeteries that New England is famous for. I loved looking at the old carvings of the headstones. The names and dates became familiar to me. The artwork was primitive. The tympanum shapes of the slate stones fascinated me to no end. I was a taphophile. That's somebody who enjoys cemeteries and the frills of a good old fashioned funeral.

As I got older and was able to drive further away from home, I began taking photographs of the old grave stones that dotted the countryside though out Massachusetts and New Hampshire. Those photo trips were before digital cameras and one was not able to see instant results. That was when the film was removed from the camera and "sent out" to be developed. A few days later, I was able to head down to the store and pick up the prints. If I was lucky, all of my photos "came out" ok. There were times that my photos had streaks in them, mist or a blurry mass. I never knew what these anomalies were. Then again, I wasn't looking for ghosts, remember, I was simply photographing headstones in colonial graveyards. I wish I had those discarded photographs now. I bet it would be quite interesting to see just what the heck I was capturing then.

Back then, all the time that I spent in the cemeteries and all the photographs that I took, regardless of what I may have been capturing were merely feeding my desire to photograph gravestones. I was, by no measure, working in the capacity of a paranormal investigator. An individual working in the paranormal field is working to collect data and trying to understand what this data is representing. Data is also called evidence. We will call data "evidence" for the remainder of this manuscript. Your goal as a paranormal investigator will be to gather good, untainted evidence and understand what it is that you are processing.

Having the right individuals working to gather this evidence will help keep it untainted. I have been very fortunate to be able to work with some of the brightest and talented investigators and mediums in the paranormal field. It wasn't always like that for me. As a matter of fact, when I decided to come out of the dark cemeteries and wanted to begin working with others in a team setting, I was blocked at every turn. I was contacting organizations that where working as "ghost hunters" and was not getting any responses back. It was discouraging to say the least, but I never gave up.

The advent of the paranormal television shows that we all know about started spawning new young "groups". The new groups on the scene were not at all "high brow" as the more in-depth paranormal researchers that did not have the patience to train a "new" person such as myself. On the same note, these T.V. shows which were being emulated by anyone with a digital camera and a voice recorder were helping to create groups of thrill seekers whose only education on the subject of the paranormal, are what they see on television, and simply mimic what they see.

Getting back to the fact that I never gave up trying to enter the paranormal field by means of getting in touch with qualified individuals was proving to be a tougher than expected process. Sure, I had worked alone in darkened cemeteries and over time had collected my tool kit. It is a very complete tool kit at that. However, it made no difference to those that I asked to take me on. Simply put, the problem wasn't that they didn't have time to respond, it was the fact that they didn't know who I was. Who was Tom Lynch? Why take a chance on an unknown. After all, you will be entering the private homes of the organizations clients. The group is responsible for the actions of each investigator on the team. You get the point of what I am saying. The thought is "We don't know you and we are all set".

I didn't give up though. I began investigating on my own. I would go to the local cemeteries and try out some techniques. If the technique that I formulated worked I incorporated it into the next "investigation". One of these techniques works so well that I named the next chapter after it. If an experimental technique did not work well, I simply stopped using it or I would keep it on the back burner and try again under different circumstances. Either way, as a good investigator, I can say that at least I tried. We will get into some of my techniques, successful or failed, throughout the chapters.

If it is your desire to get into the field via a group that is already doing investigations or you plan on starting your own team, be extremely careful of who you are lending your name to. I am a freelance paranormal investigator, not because I had given up on getting "picked up" by a team, but because I am my own teacher and I learned through countless hours of trial and error. I am way to invested in myself to take the chance of connecting myself with any one organization that can possibly fail or put out information that can ultimately be damaging to one's interests. I am not saying that I do not have a support team. I do. I have a very good team. However, the way that I have ParaTom set up is that I have built up a pool of talented, honest, like minded individuals, that have either worked with other teams in the past or individuals that I have handpicked and trained from scratch. When I need a medium, I have a medium. If I need a videographer, I have one. I know my people and I trust them to get in to the investigation and do what they were picked to do. I am always the lead investigator on a ParaTom investigation. I am always responsible for my team and my equipment. If anything goes wrong on one of my investigations, I own all of it. No questions asked. Trust everybody around you. Trust your team members. I know of a group of "investigator's" that report having over seventy five members. I'm not sure that I would be interested in a group of that size. I keep my pool at a very short number and I can tailor my investigations to suit the need for the evening. I never go in with more investigators that I need. It doesn't help the investigation at all. Look at the site of the paranormal investigation like a crime scene. Fewer bodies are better. Too many investigators can taint the evidence you are trying to collect. Again, less is better. There is a group locally who touts 30+ members. How is that a help?

OK. You have selected your team investigators and you need to come up with a name that you will go by. It needs to be a name that is easy for the public to remember. It doesn't need to be super sleek as far as theatrics. A lot of teams set up the name in hopes that Hollywood will pick them up. Don't leave the gate dreaming of your own show. Therefore name your team, not you TV show. Julie Williams and I were conducting a paranormal workshop at a local metaphysical shop when the shop owner asked if we knew an individual. She presented us with a business card for this individual and I was aspirated to read more catch phrases on that one card. One of the catch phrases was "Warrior". I immediately handed the card back and said I didn't know the individual nor was I sure I was ready to. There is no reason to be a warrior this field.

Just pace yourself. Get in, get out. Survive that first investigation and then let's see where this field takes you. If you do it all right, the rewards will come. Collect good, solid evidence. Untainted evidence is the only evidence you should be putting out there. Understand what you are collecting and when you can thoughtfully put together some sort explanation without sounding like a kid, share your findings with the world via sites like YOUTUBE, HAUNTEDTUBE and FACEBOOK.

The public will get excited about your endeavors as a paranormal investigator, but you need to know the basics. Follow a set of rules that are tried and proven. If you see a technique on TV, feel free to try it if it interests you. But do not stop there. Try it and develop it. Learn each technique inside and out. Why does it work? Why didn't it work? Experiment with all phases of the investigation until you find the procedure that works for you. I have been conducting investigations for a long time now and I do each investigation the same way each time. We do need to customize it on occasion. Not all investigations are the same; therefore, some alteration is ok as long as you follow the template. In other words, do not be jumping about and losing sight of any sort of data that may be extending itself to you and your team because you didn't follow a proven procedure. Again, will go over the ParaTom procedures in another chapter.

Ok, let's see. We've picked individuals that we know and trust. We decided if we want to start our own group or join another. We have come up with a name for the new organization and we understand the scope in which we will operate. In other words, we know our limits. Stay local or be ready to hop a flight to Dallas? Do you have the funds to support the latter? If not, your scope is operating locally. Be prepared to grow in time, and with that growth comes the opportunity to travel further outside of your scope.

Tom Lynch is working alone in a Hampstead, New Hampshire cemetery. (2007)

When you are a paranormal investigator, these doors are very inviting!

Always get the property owner's permission.

Within the walls of Riverview Cemetery in Groveland, Massachusetts

Section 2
INITIAL CONTACT WITH THE CLIENT

The day is going to come when the phone rings or you receive an email regarding a haunting. The person who is contacting you will be called a client. This client has heard about you or your group. Perhaps this client knows you already. A client can be a relative, friend or co-worker. Regardless, he or she has contacted you for a reason. It will be up to you to ask the proper questions. But, immediately, allow the client to explain the situation. A good interviewer will listen for eighty percent and talk for twenty. Ask the client to go over any information that they had reported on the initial contact. Be sure to do nothing but listen or read all the details.

The client may tell you that he or she doesn't want their spouse to know about the report. You may ask why he/she does not want the spouse to know about any pending investigations. This should put a red flag up in your head. Never consider doing an investigation if both partners are not on board. You just don't want to put yourself and your team in a situation where you need to pack up quickly and leave the investigation.

I was contacted by a woman who told me about her two hundred year old colonial home in Tewksbury, Massachusetts. She believed that she had some paranormal activity and asked if I would stop by and talk with her. I agreed to stop by and tour the home. However, I would never venture out to an interview alone with the client being of the opposite sex. One never knows what allegations can be concocted for whatever reason so I would strongly urge you to follow that same rule. Never go to a client interview alone. Bring a team member, husband or wife. Always bring somebody with you. Be safe.

Before you set up an interview and walk through, be sure you have an idea of the age of the home, who it is that owns or rents the home and if there are any pets in the house.   Try and get as much information on the property as you can. If the property has a historic name attached to it, and do a Google search on the property. You may be surprised to find old photos of the property online like I was when I looked up the Tewksbury homestead. You want to have some idea about the property before you arrive for the interview.

When the day came for my walk through in Tewksbury, I had my wife come for the ride. We arrived at the property on time and it looked completely different from the photographs I had seen online. I also knew that there was some construction done there that resulted in the front door being moved to a different location. These are things you, as an investigator, need to know. Because if you are on the investigation and you happen to see a spirit walk down the front stairs and walk through the wall, you will know it's a residual haunting and that the entity is following the original layout of the house. It walked through the wall, ok, but it was actually walking through a doorway in its' dimension.

We went to the side door and were greeted by the female homeowner, friends and some family members. I pulled out my notes and had the client recap the information that she told me on the phone. She told me that she felt the kitchen hearth area was very active but her main concern was the second story hallway and bedroom. I asked her to tell me about the activity that was happening on the second floor. She told me how she and her husband will be asleep and she is awakened, not every night, to the door closing in her seventeen year old daughter's bedroom. Then she would hear the sound of footsteps on the wide pine board floor. She would hear the steps head downstairs and hear the side door open and close. I was jotting this all down and I had the client take me upstairs and show me the area that was a concern to her. I began planning where I was going to place my infra-red DVR cameras. Surely I could get to the bottom of this.

Back down stairs, I made a big mistake. Remember I said it's ok to ask questions to gain more information? Well, I learned an important lesson that day about asking questions. I asked the woman straight out if her seventeen year old daughter had a boy friend. She replied "yes!" I then asked if it was at all possible that her daughter was sneaking the boyfriend upstairs after hours. Reasonable question, right? Doesn't matter. The interview was cut short and the woman never called me back to set up a date for the investigation. Why? Because I crossed the line. I asked a question that took the focus off the "ghost" and put it square on her daughter. Whether it was true or not, the client was put off by my suggestion, remained polite and told me that she needed to get ready for work. But again, a question that I thought was ok to ask at the time was, in hindsight, a bad question to ask any parent. Lesson learned. Keep the focus on the "ghost", not the homeowner's family members.

When you have an appointment to see the property, please be professional. If you say you are going to be there at three o'clock, get there at three o'clock. Bring a camera. Take photos of each room. Take notes as to where the family members are feeling activity. Talk to as many family members as you can during this pre-investigation interview. This is your chance to see the house in daylight that you will be investigating in the dark. With photos and notes, you will be able to prepare for the big night. You will know where to set up the cameras and other equipment.

" Do some research on the home you will be investigating!"

Be prepared to research the home you are investigating. Old photos may give clues of the original layout.

Tom works his way through the stone huts of America's Stonehenge in Salem, NH

Section Three
PREPARING FOR THE INVESTIGATION

You have met with the client and you walked through the property and got the whole scoop on just what the heck is going on there. Now, before you can move forward with the actual investigation, you need to review all your notes, the initial report and all the photo's you may have taken during the pre-investigation client interview. Before I had Julie on my staff, I needed to go over everything. Now, by the time the day of the investigation comes around, Julie has made contact a few times more with our client and we know the story and the building quite well. We have, since the walk through, discussed the case frequently. I ask Julie to double check this or that, and she gets it down. We research whatever we can locate online about the place and see if it fills any gaps, such as any past residents, deaths, births, more photographs, etc. Are there any legends or stories about the property? The stories that were told and circulated about a property have a basis somewhere in time. Researching the property will help flush the truth from the myth.

Let's take stock in the tool kit. In this field, size does not matter. A basic tool kit is a small collection of equipment that you will use during an investigation. The size of your kit may grow along with your experience. My first piece of equipment was a film camera with flash. Over time I was able to afford my first digital camera that made viewing my images instantaneous. Today I am still using a *Fuji Film Fine Pix 5200 Digital Camera*. It has enough settings on it to allow me to take night shots, basic video, etc. The thing is that I know the camera and it is easy enough to use in the dark. Take photos often. Discard nothing until you have examined each image thoroughly.

In my kit, I also have an *Olympus Digital Voice Recorder*. It is small enough fit in my pocket without issue, yet the file capacity is large enough to record an EVP (Electronic Voice Phenomena) session for up to six hours. The digital voice recorder will help you capture the surrounding ambient sounds as well as disembodied voices of the spirits around you. The digital recorder may pick up sounds being transmitted in the sound spectrum of "infra-sound". These waves are undetectable to the human ear because it is in a frequency lower than what we can naturally hear. I have picked up EVP's that sounded so clear that I was surprised that I could have missed it in real time.

This is one of my early tool kits that I keep for quick responses.

My K2 meter and digital recorder being used on an investigation

The basic *flashlight* is probably the tool that you will depend on most on an investigation. Without it, you will be fiddling in the dark, looking for your equipment or your footing. So a good flashlight is a must. With that said, carrying extra batteries on every investigation is a prudent move on your part.

I remember one time, on one of my earliest investigations; I assumed my flashlights were ready to go. I had three lights in my kit and every one of them had dead batteries. I had no extra batteries and I didn't want to look like a dope in front of the client. I sat there, not really doing much of anything because I could not see my surroundings. At that point, I was wishing that I was at home watching one of the paranormal shows on TV.

Some investigators carry a *basic compass* in their kit. In theory, if a spirit passes near the compass, the energy that it brings with it will add to or disturb the base level of the natural EMF in that area, manipulating the magnetic north of the compass and making the needle move off its' mark. I have since started carrying a compass. No batteries needed.

Another piece of equipment that I carry with me that I consider a basic tool in the kit is a *digital thermometer*. These are a good tool to have to take initial readings of the surrounding air. The readings are immediate and it is a good idea to know the temperature before and during the investigation. I was on an investigation in Marlboro, Massachusetts when I began to notice on the camera monitor, a mist passing in front of camera three. I was so excited to see and feel the results of this activity that I forgot to take a thermo reading during the event. I know the ambient temperature throughout the house was sixty eight degrees and humidity was holding at thirty percent. But it would have been an important piece of information for the sake of the investigation to see the ambient temperature drop. I felt it change, but without recording the data, one can only ring it up as a personal experience. You can surely make mention of your personal experience in the final report to the client.

Other tools that I carry in my tool kit, that I consider beyond basic, which means you can gather a bit more information about the environment in which you are investigating, but they are not necessary to execute a proper one, would be the *K2 Meter*, a device that has been made popular by the widely watched television show on the Sci-Fi channel. This device detects changes in the electro-magnetic field and reflects the change through L.E.D. lights on the device.

Another variation of the EMF detector is the *Mel Meter*. I carry this device with me on investigations because I can monitor, not just the EMF levels, but the temperature as well. This device can be set to break down the signals to very sensitive levels. It is an advanced piece of equipment.

I believe listening to a structure is very important. An investigator can get so much

The guard tower stands quiet at Eastern State Penitentiary in Philadelphia, PA

information by sitting and listening to the sounds of the building. For some situations, I carry with me, a *parabolic amplifier.* This is a super sensitive microphone with a parabolic dish connected to the microphone. This tool allows you to hear a pin drop two rooms away. The parabolic dish allows you to listen in one direction at a time. Remove the dish and you can hear the entire building at the same time.

I was lucky enough to acquire a *MSA 5200 Revolution Thermal Imaging Camera.* This is a $15,000.00 piece of equipment that allows you to see thermal signatures in absolute darkness. Now I am not one that believes ghosts can leave a heat signature, but it works great in lieu of a flashlight. It will pick up any heat source, cold spot, individual or raccoon in a dark spot without lighting up the entire area. I rarely carry it with me, but it is good to have available when needed. The TV shows enjoy using the FLIR thermal imager.

A great addition to my kit was the *ASTAK Four Channel DVR* (Digital Video Recorder). This recorder can capture four remote views from the house during the entire investigation. I bring four reels of 100' video cable to get to the furthest corners of the building without having to tie up my investigators in these areas, especially if it is a hot attic in the middle of summer.

There have been some devices that I have purchased that I wish I didn't, but, as an investigator, experimentation is a must and when I am trying something different, I feel that I am fulfilling my obligations to the client. I have used toy balls as the focal point while conducting experiments when we are trying to communicate with a child spirit.

We have discussed the basic pieces of equipment found in the tool kit. We have also discussed some advanced pieces that you do not need to conduct a quality investigation. Be sure you have at least the basics before your first investigation. You don't need to spend a million dollars to build your kit. As you gain experience, you can add to your kit.

Take time to look over the notes, photos and drawings you may have made while doing the walk thru during the client interview. Decide what you are going to bring with you, who you are bringing as support, and then what each individual on the team will be responsible for. When we are getting ready for an investigation, we know in advance where everyone will be, and what each member will be responsible for. My medium, Julie Williams, is responsible for taking notes on her impressions of the house. This is something that my equipment cannot pick up. My job is to get the homeowners situated and comfortable with our presence in the home. I am the lead investigation on all of our investigations and I need to know where everybody is at any given time during the evening. My nephew and videographer, Phil Lynch, knows that he is to be "Johnny on the spot" with the handheld digital video camera. He has been with me long enough to know where and what he is supposed to be doing. He also knows that he will be carrying in the equipment cases and running the cables for the camera system.

We all know what we are supposed to do. This gives us the appearance of being professional and knowing what we are doing and that gives the client confidence that we have this situation under control and we are not just a bunch of thrill seekers. Stay on track and be aware of the clients concerns about what will be happening in the house during the investigation. I like getting the client involved with the process and I let them know that they are welcome to join the team for the evening. I always put the K2 meter in their hand. They have seen that piece of equipment on the shows and feel they know it.

Be like a scout and *"Be prepared!"* Check your batteries; check the availability of your team members. You don't want any no-shows on the night of the investigation. Make sure you call the client and remind them of the pending investigation. Let them know that they are welcome to join the team. In my years of doing this, not a single client ever refused the invitation. It's a fun time for all of us and the client is excited to join in.

Original artwork for ParaTom.com by cartoonist Bill Swank (2009)

On the day of the investigation, have one more team meeting with your members. We hold our meeting on the way in. We go over the history, however, be careful to not give away any information that may taint your team medium(s). They do not want to know the deep specifics of the location. In that case, discuss the responsibilities of each member.

ParaTom videographer, Phil Lynch, checks his camera before the investigation.

The spirit of animals can be present at a haunting.

In this photo: A barn in New Hampshire where the spirit of a horse made itself known to the mediums.

Section Four
THE INVESTIGATION STARTS IN TEN MINUTES

You have reviewed all you're your notes and everybody knows what is expected of them. You made the appointment with the client for 7:30PM. It is important that you get there on time. The fastest way to get noticed as being unprofessional, in anything that you do is to show up late to an appointment. You set the time of the investigation. If 8:00PM is better for you and your team, then make the appointment for 8:00PM, not 7:30PM. If I sound like I am fanatical about being on time to an investigation that is because I am. I ask my investigators to be at the meeting place at a certain time. I expect them to be there. We have things to review.

You have arrived at the site of the investigation. You are dressed appropriately and so is every member of your team. A professional appearance will go a long way with the client. If you show up in ripped jeans and a t-shirt, how is the client going to have any level of confidence in your ability to help them? Do you really think the client will be comfortable with a bunch of "kids" running around their home playing ghost hunter? I will guarantee that if you dress like that going into a client's home, you will never be asked to return, nor will you get any future referrals out of them.

You knock on the door and the client opens the door and welcomes you in. Upon entering and passing the homeowner, each member of your team should acknowledge his or her presence. Thank the client for allowing you into the home. At this time, the members should be taken on a small tour of the house so they can get a feel for the layout. During the tour, ask questions or, if the client has any questions, be sure you answer them in an intelligent manner. Have the right answer for the client. The rule of "Baffle them with bull#@!t" just won't cut it this time. If you don't know the answer to the question, politely let the homeowner know that you don't have an answer at this time but you will get it as soon as possible and get back to them. The client will respect that answer better than a guess.

Depending what type of equipment you have with you, you may be ready to start the investigation sooner than later. If you have a DVR system, there are cables to run and tape down, and a monitor to hook up. The DVR needs to be set up in a central area, yet out of the way so that nobody trips on the cables and power supplies. If you do not have anything that elaborate, begin to pass out the hand equipment. If you followed my tip on discussing everybody's role prior to the investigation, they already know what equipment they will be using.

Talk with your team one more time about what will be going on this evening. Assign areas of the house to members where they will be investigating. Remember, the homeowners will take part in the investigation so assign them to a team member. Ok, the investigation starts in ten minutes. Call everybody together in a central room. Everybody in the house needs to come together in this room so that you can explain the plan for the night. Nobody is left roaming about the house. Take a second and check your equipment one more time. If you are going to allow the homeowner to use a piece of equipment, be sure they know how to properly use it. It will be a thrill for them to play investigator and they will tell all their friends about the experience, so make sure they are comfortable and are having fun during the investigation. Another suggestion to you, regarding the homeowner is that if they have any suggestions of their own as to where you should place a camera or another piece of equipment, oblige them and follow their request.

I was on an investigation where the homeowner suggested that we place a video camera at a spot in the living room, looking into the library. He told me that it was in that area that he felt like he was walking through something. I obliged his request with a camera placement. I had Phil run a cable and connect a camera head. Because I listened to the homeowner, we captured an awesome display of mist forming and rolling in front of the camera. Listen to the client. At the end of the evening, the client and his wife were happy that I listened to their suggestion. They knew house better than I did. So I listened. And it paid off in more ways than one. Lesson learned: Listen and don't come across like you know better than the homeowner. I guarantee that it will leave a bad taste in their mouth. If you do listen, you will have made valuable contacts for future investigations.

The investigation is about to start. Let the home owners know that you need all the lights off in the house. Be sure that every member of the investigation has a flashlight. All cell phones MUST BE powered off. Not simply put on silence. That includes the home telephones. Are there any parts of the home that are to be considered off limits? Be sure that all the members of your team understand the areas marked "off limits". Pets should be placed in an area marked off limits for the entire investigation. There is nothing worse than having a dog barking continuously while you are trying to conduct an investigation. It would be a good idea to have the home owner drop the dog or cat off at a family members house for the night. Lights Out!

Original Drawing by Bill Swank for ParaTom.com (2009)

Nothing paranormal here! Faulty grounding to copper piping causes this K2 Meter to react.

"All cell phones MUST BE powered off."

Section Five
TWENTY MINUTES OF SILENCE

The lights are out so what do you do now? If you are on a ParaTom investigation, the answer is simple. No talking for twenty minutes. Say what? I said "no talking for twenty minutes". Ok. Let me explain that rule. And it is a rule that I have adhered to for quite awhile, because it helps the quality of the investigation on a few levels.

When I was working alone in this field, I was able to try without different techniques without risk. If a technique did not work, I could simply change it or drop it all together. The *twenty minute rule* comes from the days when I would sit in old cemeteries at night, sitting there and using my ears rather than my eyes. I noticed that when I would close my eyes, my ears almost became bionic. That is to say, my ears became more sensitive to sound when my eyes were not adding stimulation to the brain. When I used to hunt, I found myself using this technique to hear the approach of a deer. I didn't use my eyes until I heard a deer coming my way. I wasn't much of a shot, so I learned to just sit there and enjoy the sounds of the forest. So it was a good fit for my paranormal investigations.

Just before the last light in the house goes out, be sure your team is asked to get into a comfortable position. I don't care if you are sitting down, laying down on your back or on your stomach or standing on your head, but whichever position you choose, you stay like that for twenty minutes. No scratching your leg, moving your feet or blowing your nose. The purpose of this exercise is twofold. The first is that it allows the team to get accustomed to the sounds of the house. Lay back and close your eyes. Just listen to the ambient sounds that the house is putting out to you. You may hear the hum of the furnace or the air conditioner may pop on or the house may crack and pop as it settles. What you are listening for is everything to repeat. At the end of the twenty minutes, you should know every sound that the house makes. If, after twenty minutes, you hear a new sound that you didn't hear earlier, then that is what you want to figure out. It could be something that had a longer recycle time. Investigate that sound.

The second reason we use the twenty minutes of silence on an investigation is it is beneficial to my mediums that need to tune into the environment. We all just do better when we take twenty minutes to sit and listen. Try that on your investigations and I promise you better results.

Another rule that I adhere to is that no perfumes or colognes are to be worn on a ParaTom investigation. The reason for this is simple. Our clients tell us may tell us that they get a smell of a woman's perfume at midnight. It smells of lilacs. It smells like the kind here deceased granny wears. We want some of that action. It will only be a personal experience and nothing that can be recorded. But we want to smell the lilac perfume regardless. But if Phil decides to show up on the investigation smelling of AXE Body Spray, then the field is contaminated and we will not get the chance to smell Grannies' lilac perfume. Get it?   No perfumes on the investigation. Let the home owner know this technique in advance of the investigation so they do not run the risk of contaminating the investigation. Shut all cell phones OFF.

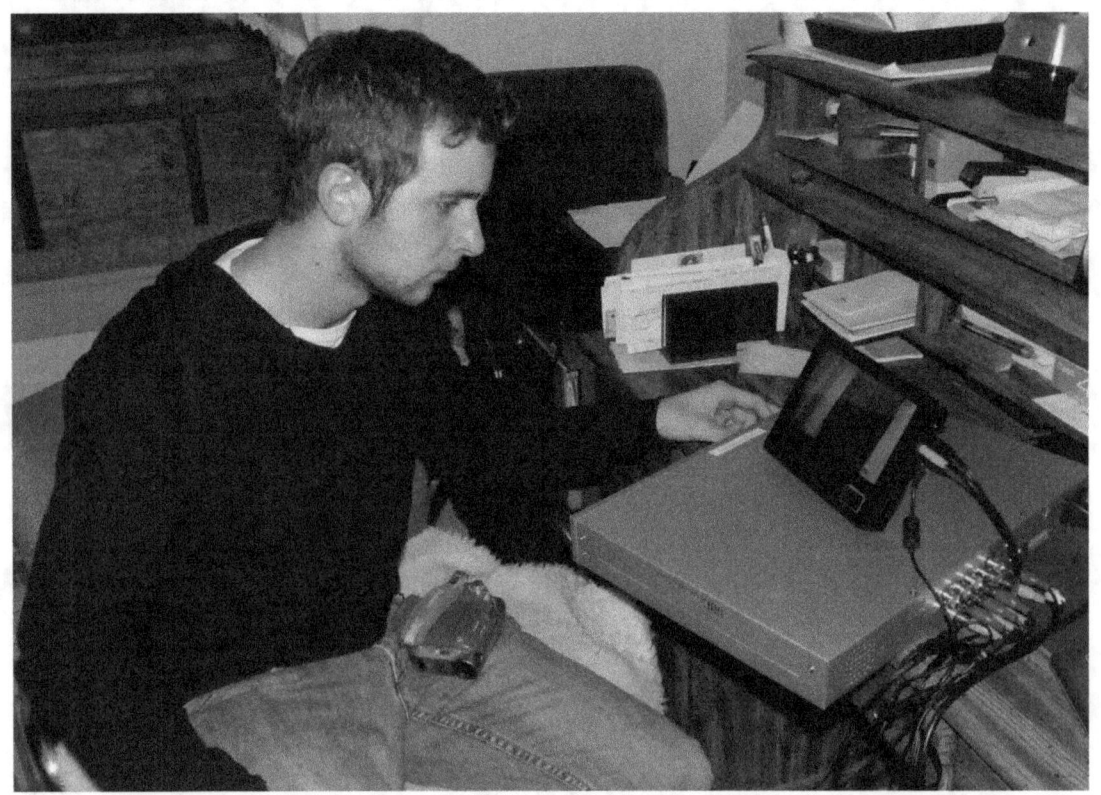

In this photo: Phil is watching the monitor for any paranormal activity.

Section Six
STAY TOGETHER OR SPLIT UP

The twenty minutes is just about up and do you have any idea what you want to tackle next? And how do you want to do it? Do you want to break up into smaller teams or do you want to do it together? When I ask that question, it depends on the size of the team that I have assembled for that evening. If I have enough investigators on hand, I have no issue splitting up the team. If I have two mediums on hand, then each team has the luxury of a medium.

We head to our designated areas, keeping in mind, the areas that have been marked "off limits." If you have reviewed your notes and photographs taken during the initial walk through, then you already have an idea of where you want to place your teams. Nobody should be in an unfamiliar area alone. With that said, a team should be made up of a minimum of two investigators. No more than four members. Any more than that in any situation can cause a tainting of the area and captured data.

We break up into teams for a few reasons. The first is to allow an area to remain relatively controlled by minimal activity by the investigative teams. If you have ever been on a large "pay to get in" investigation, than you know how frustrating it is to be in an area with laughter, whispering, unnecessary movement and shuffling can be. Julie and I were invited onboard the U.S.S. Salem, docked in Quincy Harbor, in Massachusetts. A local group was putting on a fund raiser for the battleship and asked us to tag along. We were hoping to get some time to conduct our level of investigation, but once upon the vessel, our hopes were dashed. There was just way to many tourists on board that wanted to "investigate". We were told we had to stay with our assigned group and there would be no wondering about the ship. We retired our thoughts of a serious investigation of the U.S.S. Salem and simply enjoyed the tour.

"Nobody should be in an unfamiliar area alone."

Tom Lynch and Julie Williams pose with clients during a Derry, New Hampshire investigation in 2009

There were just too many people scurrying about to be able to do any type of investigation.

There are times where a large group is permitted. The first instance is during twenty minutes of silence. Everybody is seated and comfortable in a main area. You are listening to the ambient sounds of the structure. The only time that this session should be divided, is if you are investigating a large building such as a hospital or warehouse. Other than that, in a home or small building, everybody stays together and just listens. The second instance would be when the lead investigator wants to conduct a K2 session or another form of communication and wants the unit as a whole to attend. Again, once together for such a demonstration, the team needs to settle and have no unnecessary moving about or talking, unless asked by the lead investigator to ask questions. Other than that, the rule is no talking or shuffling. I don't want to come across as a hard ass on the subject of silence or movement, but we are on scene to try and capture evidence of paranormal activity.

We were on an investigation in Derry, New Hampshire and as lead investigator for the evening; I wanted to gain control of the large colonial home immediately. We had four investigators and three residents for a total of seven individuals on the scene. We all settled in the living room and began our twenty minutes of silence. After which, we split up into our pre-determined teams. During the investigation, Phil and his video camera was bouncing between the two teams. He was able to capture the teams performing their EVP sessions and other forms of communication and detection. He was basically the only investigator "authorized" to be moving between teams at that time.

After being split up for the first half of the investigation, I called the teams together in the "blue room" on the second floor. This was the room that was reportedly the area of the house where an image of a woman dressed in colonial period clothing was videotaped when the homeowner and his daughter had gone out for the evening. Once assembled, we all got comfortable and settled in and began an EVP and K2 sessions. After this session the entire unit headed downstairs to the dining room and conducted a "Franks Box" session. This was not just an experiment in communications with the spirits of the home, but it also gave me the means to demonstrate these sessions to the homeowners and newer team members that may never actually attended such a session.

Deciding to stay or breakup into smaller teams depends then on how many team members you have on the investigation and the size of the area being investigated. You should be able to determine who you have available for the investigation a week in advance. You have seen the size of the building when you met with the client and did a walk through. Therefore, you should have been mentally making notes during that time to figure out how many investigators you were going to use and if you, as lead investigator, were going to sub-divide the unit.

Never take more investigators than you need. There are times where two investigators are plenty. The larger the investigation site, the more bodies you may use. But I would never want to use more than six investigators on any given event. The proper number of investigators will help assure some sort of control during the investigation.

If you are using teams, be sure that each team rotates throughout the building. Each team should settle at the designated hot spots. This rotation will allow each team to experience any activity as well as compare notes on experiences, personal or captured, at the conclusion of the investigation.

Here is the bottom line about staying together or breaking up into smaller teams during an investigation. It is up to you to decide if it will be a controlled, yet thorough investigation. I feel that less is better. If you are going to do it right, learn to determine how many investigators will be used BEFORE you arrive at the scene. It's all about gathering clean, untainted evidence that can be scrutinized repeatedly without finding any outside interference.

"...be sure that each team rotates throughout the building."

Never venture out alone in unfamiliar locations. This stairway is deep within Buffalo Central Terminal. A careless investigator could easily get lost within its' walls.

Section Seven
GATHERING EVIDENCE

We have arrived at the very heart of why we are conducting a paranormal investigation. We want to be able to capture untainted data, or evidence. It will be your goal as a paranormal investigator, to try and coax out of the environment, any amount of clean proof that there may be something going on in the building that may or may not be disproved. When I am conducting an investigation, I am going into it as somewhat of a skeptic. That is not to say that I do not believe in paranormal activity because God knows that I have experienced my share of this stuff. As weird as some of the "activity" is, I can tell you that about ninety eight percent of it can be disproven, or as they say on the popular TV shows, debunked. What about the other two percent? Well, let's just say that two percent is what keeps me interested in the field.

My very first investigation was not really an investigation at all. It was more of an inquisitive review of an activity that had happened moments earlier. When I am touring, I refer to this event as "Uncle Lucien's Bell". My wife's great uncle Lucien was an elderly man who was living with her grandparents around the mid to late Eighty's. Well, old Uncle Lucien was very ill and his health was declining. So much so, that he needed to breathe through a tube cut into his throat. This in turn, took away the ability to speak at all and was given a little brass bell to ring when assistance was needed. Well one day, Lucien passed away, peacefully in the bed, on the second floor of the house on Charles Street, Methuen, Massachusetts.

We buried Lucien on a clear day and it was that evening that my wife and I decided to sit in with her grandparents, Annette and Charlie. There were four adults in that house that evening. We were all watching television together when, all of a sudden, we heard a bell ringing from upstairs. Charlie and I headed upstairs and as we got closer to the source, the ringing was getting louder. It was acoustically correct and directional. As I touched the doorknob of Lucien's room, the ringing stopped. We were dumbfounded by this episode. We all have our "ah ha" moment, that was mine.

Something definitely happened to cause that bell to ring. It was sitting on the television near the bed. Here is the instant of my first paranormal "investigation". I gently picked up the brass bell, tested the tone, which was exactly what we heard and looked at the thin layer of dust on the television to determine if any drag marks were left behind from whatever caused that bell to ring. There was nothing on the surface that appeared to be disturbed. The bell sat on the TV, which created a faint spot void of any dust, visible only when I lifted the bell. I never did figure that one out. But as an investigator, I do revisit it in my head quite a bit.

Let's take a look at that experience and try to figure out a game plan. You are about to enter into an investigation that has reported activity such as a bell ringing. What would you want to do about trying to catch the activity as evidence?

Despite the clutter of a home, care must be taken not to disturb anything, including dust. Dust will cause "orbs" and create false evidence.

"...all of a sudden, we heard a bell ringing from upstairs".

No matter the size of the house, hallways seem to be a hot zone for paranormal activity.

I would suggest that a team be placed within the area of the reported activity. It may occur again. It may not. Did others witness this activity in the past? What were the conditions at the time? You ask these questions to determine if the haunting is actively trying to get your attention (an intelligent haunting) or a residual haunting. That is a haunting which is the result of stored energy within a space. It can be better compared to a tape recording that has been looped. The team assigned to that area needs just sit and wait to see if during the evening, the bell ringing happens again. In this case, patience is a virtue.

Not all teams have the luxury of, or even would want to have a sub team sit out the rest of the investigation with the slim chance of catching this event. As a matter of fact, it would be nothing more than a personal experience that would only serve as mental fodder years from now, as it cannot be shared with anyone else. To remedy this issue, your tool kit should have at least a couple of digital voice recorders that can be placed in remote areas of the premises. These recorders will free up your investigators to pursue other facets of the investigation.

The use of the MSA5200 Thermal Imager is used in lieu of a flashlight on some investigations.

Another tool for remote investigative sessions would be the handheld video camera with "night vision" capabilities as well as the multi-channel Digital Video Recorder (DVR). The ParaTom Investigative Unit uses a four channel system that can remotely view outlaying areas of the premises. By obtaining a DVR system for your organization, you will be able to view several areas while monitoring from one central area, thus keeping your investigators free to investigate all locations of the site.

"The team assigned to that area needs just sit and wait..."

The ParaTom Investigative Unit uses the Astak 4 Channel DVR system for viewing remote areas.

Handheld video recorders are a great tool for any investigation. WNY Ghost Hunters member, Yvonne records Tom at BCT, NY.

Remote viewing would be ideal for this basement of an old Jewish temple in N.Y. which the ParaTom Investigative Unit investigated in 2009.

In this photo: Tom visiting Buffalo Central Terminal in Buffalo, NY (2009)

The whole premise of conducting an investigation is to gather evidence that will support the existence of a reported haunting. It is the responsibility of an investigative unit to use any and all equipment available to capture and collect data, understand it, and keep it confidential, until the client has been able to view it. It would be risky to put something out in front of the public and make a firm statement as to what it is and then have it disproven. You just lost your credibility by those who had to go in and "fix" your statement. Never put your team or yourself in that position. Taking notes is an important part of any investigation. Some of the information you want to record is the ambient temperature and the humidity level. You also want to make note of the time, especially when you are changing locations or starting an EVP or K2 session. It just helps keep track of the physical conditions during the onset of a session, field experiment or location change. When recording an entry, you can simply write:

"9:45PM: Tom Lynch moving from living room to dining room. Ambient temperature 67 degrees with a humidity level of 37%. Beginning EVP session, dining room".

Again, by recording this information, you begin to build a correlation to when, where and why activity happens. This can all be useful information over time when you begin to compare activities from different investigations. I conducted an investigation in Marlboro, Massachusetts in November of 2010 with an event that was spectacular. My DVR system captured a burst of mist that seemed to appear out of nowhere. My staff medium, Julie Williams, with naked eye, was seeing a black shapeless form appear at the very spot that my camera was capturing. She described the form as "coming from out of nowhere and moving down the hall and into the room that Tom was in, and then disappeared". By taking note of the time, temperature and humidity, I was able to add in my report to the client that this event happened at 8:30PM with an ambient temperature of sixty eight degrees and a humidity level of thirty percent.

This may not sound like anything important right now, but say we have eight more such events with a mist that seems to form out of nowhere. We will be able to compare our notes with other organizations. We may find a correlation between time, temperature and humidity levels. That is where the research begins. To research a finding, one must be ready to experiment during an investigation. Take your notes, formulate a reasonable experiment and try to capture some like results.

EVP's are a great way to capture some useable evidence. Try placing some voice recorders around the premises and leave them undisturbed. Place the recorders in reported hotspots and see what you get. You may be surprised. Faking EVP's or any other evidence does not do an ounce of good, but a pound of bad. So please, don't do it. Good evidence will come. Maybe the first time out. Maybe not. It is only on TV that things happen every time. There were nights that I wished I was at home watching those television investigators instead of being in a dank basement of a chilly old homestead. Guarantees are far and few between in this field. Be patient. It will happen.

Do not add anything to your evidence that you capture. I.e. titles, voiceovers, etc. That's not to say you cannot clean up a photo or a recording for viewing or listening. However, keep the original, untouched version in a safe location. Do not widely distribute any evidence until the client has had a chance to review it. We always supply the client with a CD or DVD of the captured evidence. Along with that, we give them a printed report with a rundown of the night's activity, the names of the investigators on hand and notes from the mediums that I had on board for the evening. It gives the full picture of the evening.

Original photo

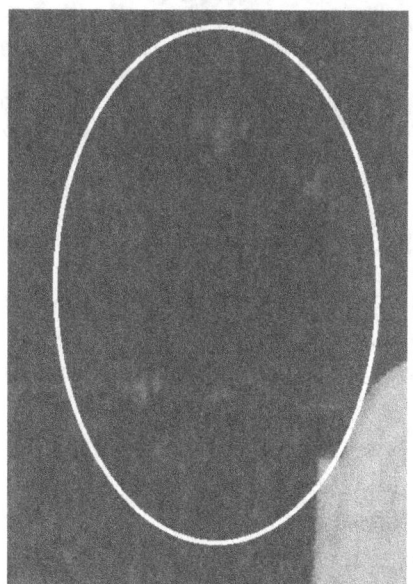

Enlargement

This is a piece of evidence recorded while Julie and I were photo gathering. What is it?
It appears to be the ghostly form that was captured in a local cemetery. (2010)

False evidence: This photo is the result of a slow shutter speed. Julie appears to be fading away. (2010)

I have been asked many times to describe what good evidence is. What should it look like? My reply is always "…you never know what you're going to get". Is good evidence any better than bad evidence? In this field, evidence is evidence. Good or bad. But it is either true or false.

We try different tactics to collect any recordable evidence as we can. We conduct EVP sessions. We set out video cameras and "Frank's Boxes, Mel meters and K2 meters. Some investigators use the "Puck" or the Ovilus. Whether any of these devices work better than others depends on the investigation and the energy that you are dealing with. I know of a man who claims his only piece of equipment is a basic compass. That will allow you to see results, but how can he get beyond a personal experience? No video of the activity would be available for discussion, dissection or examination.

Evidence is shared in many forms. Video, voice recordings (EVP), photographs and meter readings. However, it is the first three that you will be able to examine long after the investigation is over. The meter readings are dependent on your credibility.

In this photo: Subject looks like he is being followed. In reality, my slow shutter speed captured the glow of his own digital camera's LCD screen as he walked forward. Looks ghostly though!

This hallway in the Edith Wharton Estate stables was the location of a disembodied "sigh".
As I investigated this area, a "sigh" was heard at two feet out from my front right.

I love disproving photos like the one on the previous page. When I first took the photo of the man in the basement, I knew immediately what had occurred in the photo and why. I posted the photo on Face Book just because it was a good looking shot. I knew there was nothing paranormal there, but I got so many explanations of what it was, from "reflections of white walls to reflections of light off windows, theories abound. Good guesses all around, but as a professional investigator, I knew it was a slow shutter speed and a bright LCD screen on the subjects' digital camera. Learn to know what is going on with your photos.

Toms uses a mag light and compass on a headstone during an experiment.

To reiterate the reason for this chapter in the book, it is to gather evidence with the help of digital cameras, video cameras, and voice recorders. These basic pieces of equipment will allow you to "capture" any activity that you may encounter and review and share it.

The other pieces of equipment in the tool kit, such as a K2 meter, Mel Meter, compass, Franks Box or Shack Hack will allow you to illustrate the presence or onset of any activity. Unless you are video recording these pieces of equipment, there is no way of actually obtaining the data that they provide. The Mel Meter can record and store some data, but nothing that can be uploaded and shared.

If you are investigating, using a flashlight and your senses only, which are absolutely fine, you are investigating with the hopes of capturing "personal experiences" only. You can never share these experiences with others. That is, you will be able to tell them about the experience, but you will never be able to upload, share, study, or review the personal experience.

Despite any piece of equipment you may be in possession of, be sure you understand how to use it long before you investigate with it. Batteries need to be checked prior to the investigation. Carry extra batteries with you. Batteries can go dead immediately after the on start of certain paranormal activity.

Society has softened its view on the paranormal after the advent of the TV shows. In this photo, Karl and Harry chat with Tom and Julie on the set of "Spektral Evidence."

The sole reason you are investigating a haunting, is to gather information, data, or evidence. Be sure that if you are looking to share the experiences, you have at least some sort of recordable equipment with you.

When investigating, I like to try some experimentation to see if I can develop new ways of coaxing the ghosts out of the woodwork. I have used balls to UV lighting in my experiments. Do they produce any more or less activity? That is not the point. The point is that you, while gathering information, experimented. You theorized a probable result. We will cover experimentation in the next chapter. For now, be careful with the "evidence" of paranormal activity. Do not share it with others outside of your team until you can fairly understand what it actually may be. A "mist" on a winter's day may be the cameraman's breath. I said "may be". Understand your evidence.

"The sole reason you are investigating a haunting, is to gather information, data, and evidence."

Section Eight

CONDUCTING FIELD EXPERIMENTS

I have done many experiments while in the field. These field experiments are important to the development of new techniques and procedures. By now, you know that I am a fan of the "No talking for twenty minutes" procedure. This procedure came about when I used to sit in cemeteries alone at night. The closing of the eyes can produce a better way of listening. Your ears become come super sensitive when the eyes are taken out of the equation. That's not to say that you won't be able to look around during the investigation. I am saying that the first twenty minutes will be dedicated to hearing what the surroundings are throwing out at you. I use this procedure on every investigation that I conduct. It seems to work well and gives us a solid starting point for the investigation.

As a spinoff benefit of this procedure, not only is it giving us the chance to take in all the ambient sounds of the surroundings, my mediums report that they are able to use that twenty minutes to also ground themselves and connect with the energy within the premises. This procedure came about because I experimented with my own senses.

That was only an example of how procedures and techniques are written for this field in which we work. As I develop these guidelines, my investigations get somewhat tighter. That is to say, my investigations become smoother in execution and we can begin to know how we will use our resources and time. This in turn, shows the client that we have used our time wisely in developing our program and have not wasted any of theirs.

Besides the experimentation of procedure, we look to the experimentation of technique. We, as investigators, need to be able to draw on our experiences to draw out and capture any activity that may help us understand the haunting at any scale. Some is better than nothing. It is important that your team has techniques in place for certain situations.

Julie and I were in Windham, New Hampshire in November of 2010, participating in a multi-team investigation of a historic home that was full of history. We understood that we may encounter the spirit of a little boy in a second floor bedroom. This was the perfect opportunity to experiment while trying to communicate with the spirit. Knowing about the spirit of the little boy in advance, I brought with me a rubber ball smaller than a tennis ball but very light in weight. Once up in the second floor bedroom, I took out the ball and placed it on the wide pine floor board. Julie and I began an EVP session as we would always do, but this time, with the rubber ball out, we asked the spirit to go ahead and play with the ball. "Can you move the ball with any means possible?" "Just move the ball slightly and we will be able to see it". We asked the spirit of the little boy to try his best to move the ball. We chose a ball for this experiment because it was reasonable to assume that it would be able to recognize a ball from his time here on earth.

The ball never did move, but who is to say this experiment would never work in the future? So, even though we got no movement of the ball that night, we plan on using that technique in future investigations that involve the spirit(s) of children. That night, the spirit was able to follow some basic instructions and as a result, it was able to keep the ball even after we left.

When dealing with a child spirit, we want to talk with a soft, nurturing voice. We want to entice it with a toy. We want to gain its trust, just like the way we would handle a child in life. The experiment did not yield any results that night, but we did experiment. Sometimes things work out, most times they don't, but we fulfilled our duties as investigators.

The use of the ball has been used on television programs and by other investigators in the past. I am not the originator of this technique, but we did use it and will continue to use it. Other experiments can be used as well. I always pictured a simple paper device that can be manipulated by the residual energy of a spirit. This is electro-magnetic energy that we, as living beings possess. All living creatures emit a very small amount of electric energy which can be viewed with Kirlian photography. This is a technique that demonstrates its principle.

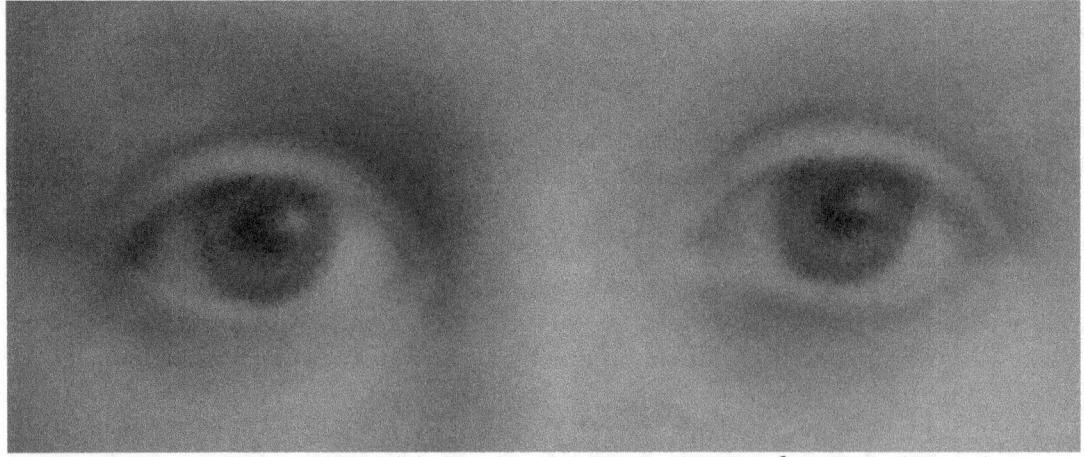

"When dealing with a child spirit, we want to talk with a soft, nurturing voice."

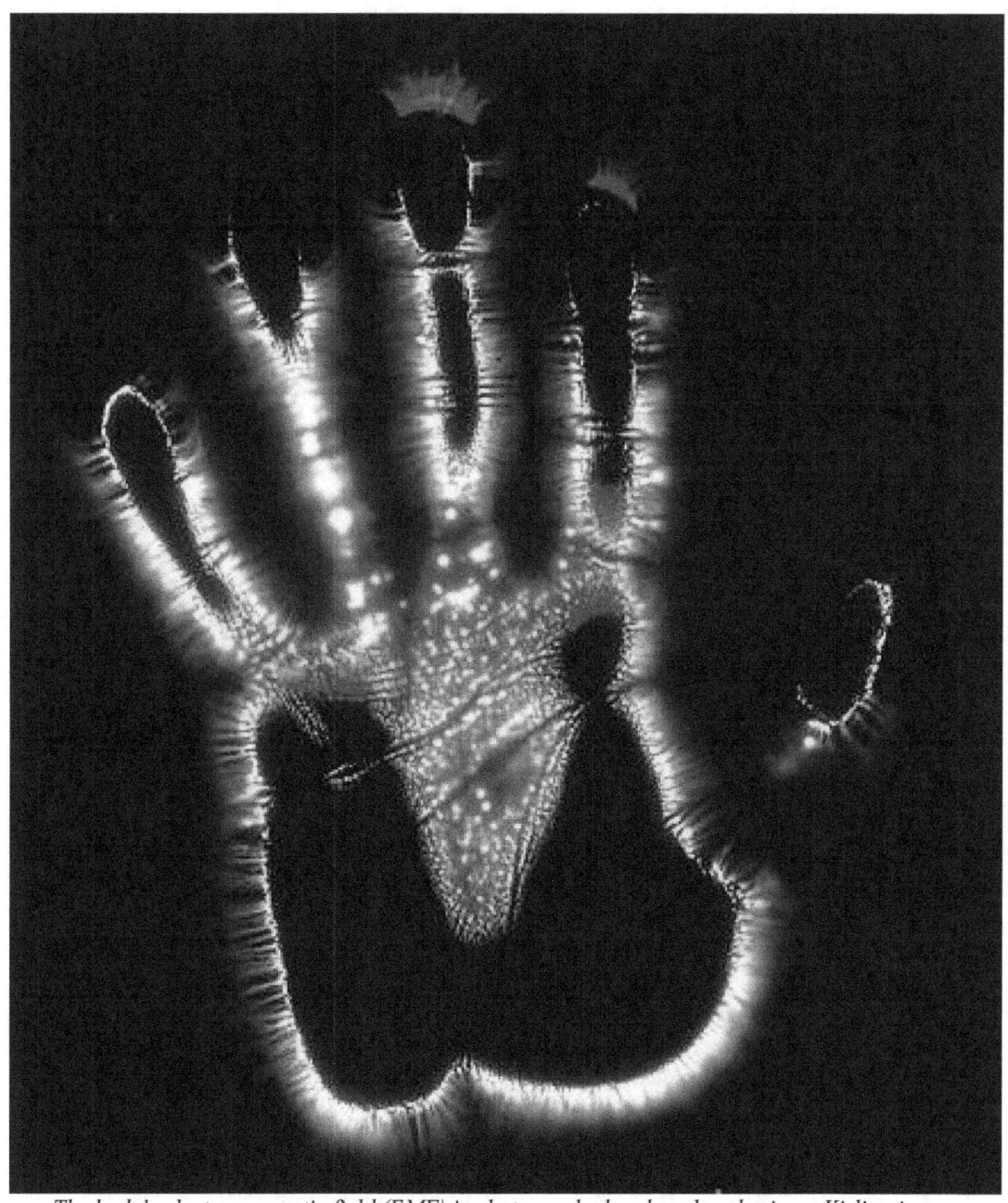

The body's electro-magnetic field (EMF) is photographed and analyzed using a Kirlian image.

✓ Learn more about Kirlian imagery online.

45

EXPERIMENT ZONE

TRY THIS: Get and cut a piece of wax paper about one inch square. Fold the paper as shown in the photograph. That is, diagonal corner to corner. This will create a raised center. With a push pin as the center pole, sit the paper on the pin. It should be balanced. The idea of this experiment is that the paper is lightweight and should be able to spin easily on the head of the pin.

We all have electrical energy flowing out and away from us. Theoretically, energy can effectively spin the paper. Practice this by placing your hands around the paper without touching it. Concentrate on spinning the paper. It should, with practice, spin on the pin.

Spirits are made up of this residual energy. During an investigation, ask the spirit to approach the paper and see it can spin it or knock it off the pin. Any movement will be detectible. I place my paper "device" in a jar so that air movement doesn't create false activity.

The simple device that I use is a square piece of light weight, stiff paper that is about one and a half inches square and fold corner to diagonal corner, making an X crease in the paper. The center of the square is slightly raised now and sits on a push pin. Balance the paper on the tip of the pin. It should balance nicely on the pin. Place your finger tips near the device. Place them on either side. With practice, and concentration, you should be able to get the paper to spin due to the energy rushing from the tips of your fingers. It took a while, but I can now do it now easily. Once you master it yourself, consider bringing it on an investigation and have it set up in an area free from draft or breeze and invite a spirit to try it. Who knows, it just might start spinning.

Be sure to be video recording the experiment. I have yet to bring this paper device on an investigation, but I have, at the time of this writing, renewed my promise to do so. Again, what I am trying to do is motivate you to experiment. Whether it works or not, experiment. At least you tried. No gains are made in the field if you don't experiment. Can you formulate some sort of an experiment that you would like to try in the field during an investigation? Let's see if we can formulate an experiment that we can use during an investigation.

THEORY: It is reported that ghosts drain the batteries of our flashlights or digital cameras to gain energy to materialize or communicate with us. What can we do to test that theory?

EXPERIMENT: We can set out flashlights and see if the spirit will use the energy, or maybe we can alter that experiment a bit and add a larger battery with more energy for the spirit to use. Just for fun, let's use a car battery and a 12V auto bulb. The light bulb will get the energy flowing, making it available for the spirit. That should be enough energy to have a ghost or two materialize, or at least get a cold spot.

EXPECTED RESULT: We would hope to see the bulb eventually go dim as the entity "steals" the energy of the larger battery. This, in turn, would lend itself to the idea that ghosts, taking energy from the surrounding air and other sources, would create a cold spot and then materialize.

Would this experiment work? Theoretically, yes! But the point is that we would never know if we do not experiment. Data goes hand in hand with experimentation. Earlier in the body of this book, I wrote that data will not make sense at the onset of collecting it, but would begin to show its' importance when further collections of the same information are compared. The use of your K2 meter, voice recorder, video camera and other equipment from your tool kit is quite acceptable during experimentation. Be sure that you take notes. Be sure that you make note of the ambient air temperature as well as humidity levels and time of day. Weather? What equipment did you use? What are the results of your experiment?
Try this experiment in different conditions, on different investigations and see if anything "materializes".

To end this chapter, I just want to say that anything goes! Don't be afraid to try relevant and intelligent experiments. If it fails, so what. You tried. If it works and you get positive results...Great! The experiment worked. Use it on some investigations.

Another experiment I have conducted was that of introducing mist into a photograph to see what may be captured. Take a look over Julie's right shoulder. Do you see the ghostly face, mouth open?

"Be sure you take notes".

Section Nine
WRAPPING UP THE INVESTIGATION

The investigation is coming to an end. During the client interview, you may have agreed to a time in which the interview would finish up. Be sure that you are mindful of the time throughout the investigation. Time flies when you're having fun and that is especially true when you are conducting a quality investigation. I have been on investigations that nothing was happening and I found myself looking at my watch every ten minutes, hoping that something paranormal would push the hands of my watch forward by three hours. However, I am glad to say that as I have added certain procedures and techniques to my investigations, I seldom want that time to end.

At the appropriate time, ask the homeowner to turn the lights back on. At this time, have everybody, homeowners and investigators, gather their handheld equipment and bring it back to the central area. It will be your responsibility to make sure all the equipment is accounted for before you leave the clients home. Know what was handed out before the investigation began.

Once everybody is accounted for, have everybody take a seat and begin a debriefing session. This should last anywhere from ten to thirty minutes. This time will allow everybody that was present to share their experiences, personal or recorded. Have somebody video the debriefing or take hand written notes. This will give you some source of information to draw from when completing the client report. When I am completing an investigation, I leave plenty of time for the debriefing. You never know what may come up.

On the investigation in Marlboro, Massachusetts, we completed all the tasks that we set out to perform. At that time, I called all team members back to the living room where we started the investigation. I asked everybody to get comfortable and we began to go over the evenings events. Of course, the footage of the mist that was caught on the DVR was the focal point. However, we wanted to discuss everybody's experiences. My mediums compared their impressions of the entities that they have been aware of since they walked into the room. The homeowners, both sensitive, concurred with what my mediums, Julie and Deb, were reporting. This adds credibility to our services rendered.

At the end of this investigation, Phil listens in at the debriefing. (2009)

"... have everybody take a seat and begin a debriefing session."

Staff Medium, Lori Hand and the property owners watch the monitor at the end of the investigation.

Lori and Phil of ParaTom.com listen in at a debriefing.

Hopefully, you were able to complete every facet of the investigation that you set out to accomplish. The worst thing you can do is tell the client that you were not able to complete the task that you told them you can perform. The only time this should ever happen is when the client needs to end the investigation for whatever reason. Hopefully they did not stop the investigation because you went beyond the agreed time. Let me list the steps or tasks we should be concentrating on during an investigation. Keep this list with you as it will come in handy while debriefing your team at the end of an investigation.

1) *Proper Placement of your equipment.*

2) *Twenty minutes of silence.*

3) *Proper placement of your teams.*

4) *EVP sessions in all hot spots.*

5) *K2 or EMF meter sessions in all hot spots.*

6) *Video recording of all areas of the investigation.*

7) *Photography of all areas of the investigation.*

8) *Experimentation of any sort. Just experiment.*

9) *Debriefing session and review of events.*

Those are the nine basic steps of an investigation that are conducted at the sight of an investigation. The final two steps are conducted after the actual on-site investigation is over. These steps are:

10) *Review and upload ALL evidence recorded.*

11) *Report back to the client with evidence and written report in a timely manner.*

Follow these eleven steps and you will conduct a quality investigation. Miss one step and you may run the risk of missing some important evidence, or worse, hurt your credibility as a diligent paranormal investigator. Clients want to know that you are on the ball and that you are taking their situation and concerns seriously and responsibly. While we are on the subject of what the client expects from you, I failed to mention this at the beginning of the book. You must handle all client information, including their initial report, with respect and confidentiality. Unless they give you permission to use their situation and their likeness, i.e. photos or video, you will not be able to share their story or photographs with anyone outside of your organization.

With that said, let's take a look at the wrap up of the investigation. This was an exciting experience for your clients. They were able to take part in a paranormal investigation. Hopefully you were able to capture some great evidence for them to review after you have reviewed it all. They wait with anticipation to hear what you had to say about their haunting. Be prepared during the briefing to explain to the client what the team had experienced. Do not be afraid to let them know if the door upstairs opens when someone walks on a loose floor board. It will serve the client better if they know the truth.

If the closet door upstairs was cited as part of the haunting and your team members disproved it as loose floor board that raises the door jamb and dislodges the locking mechanism and causes the door to open, then demonstrate that to the client. They may be disappointed at the debunking, but finding an EVP will recharge their excitement.

Before you leave the premises, be sure you explain to the homeowners what the next step is. You will be going over all the voice recordings, photographs and video footage. Remember that for every minute that you recorded audio and video, it will be minute for minute of review. So, don't promise them a turnaround time of your findings in an unrealistic time frame. I tell my clients to expect something back, in the form of a typed out report and DVD, in about two weeks. If I get it back to them before then, everybody is happy. If I get the packet back to them after the deadline, I may be damaging my reputation as a professional.

Be sure you have accounted for all of your equipment. If you have a multi-channel DVR, be sure you roll up the cables and take up all the tape that secured the cables down so nobody on the investigation tripped. Get your team ready to leave. The equipment is in the vehicle and it's time to say goodbye. Let the client know that you will get on the task of reviewing all the footage and files as soon as possible and you will get back to them with a packet. Explain what will be in the packet so they will not be expecting anything more than what you agreed to. If you have some business cards with you, which I recommend you do, hand the client a few and ask them to hand them out. If you did your job properly, they will be happy to accept them and pass them out to their friends and family who may also have activity.

As each team member leaves the premises, they are to thank the client for the opportunity to help. Remind the client that you will be in touch in the near future.

Tom visiting Eastern State Pen, Philadelphia.

Tom recording a radio spot for TCP Radio at Fort Mifflin, Philadelphia as Bill Horton looks on. (2009)

This artwork seemed oddly at home within the walls of Buffalo Central Terminal in Buffalo, NY (2009)

The long dark hallways of Buffalo Central Terminal are no joke to an inexperienced investigator.

Section Ten

GIVING IT BACK TO THE CLIENT

The investigation is over. You had a great evening. It was exciting and there will be a lot to talk about on the ride home. But is the investigation complete? Not yet! Now the real work begins. Hours of review, minute for minute, you will relive every minute of the investigation, that is to say, if you have a DVR system that was running the entire time. For each minute that was recorded, for each channel that was recorded, for each piece of equipment you used to record the investigation, multiply that by the time you now need to go over everything. And when I say everything, I mean everything. You need to watch and listen with diligence. You need to concentrate on every single second of your review and make notes of the time and location of each occurrence that you feel is important to the investigation.

The client had contacted you to do a thorough investigation of their premises. You are sure that you rendered a service to the level of their expectations. Let that be equally evident in this phase of the case as well. Do not take shortcuts. I know a lot of investigators that "fast forward" through hours of video just to have missed something of importance.

Paranormal or not, if the event will help settle the concerns of the property owner, discover it, review it, understand it and then, include it in the final report. Try to either properly disproving the event as non-paranormal or, if no other explanation is appropriate, being sure you discuss it fully with qualified team members or an outside authority. Never be in a hurry to put your reputation on the line by making the claim that an event is paranormal until you fully understand it, or until you have discussed and reviewed it with an outside third party.

When you have reviewed all the material from the investigation, you need to put all your findings in an easy to follow format for the client. I include a written report and a DVD or CD for the client to keep. By presenting these items in a packet, it lends itself to a professional presentation. And that is what the client expects and deserves.

I always include printed reports from my mediums that were on the investigation. This way, the property owners can understand the spiritual aspect of the investigation as well. I have my team write up their own reports with their perspectives of the incidents that they witnessed. I try to avoid hearsay in the reports. I trust my mediums because I know them and I know their capabilities. The information that they provide is helpful to fill in the spaces that my equipment had left behind. This in turn, helps gives the client a well rounded view of the investigation and the findings of the team. I conclude the written portion of our packet with my own take on each event, including what was reported to me by my investigators. To be able to get the packet back to my clients, I always set a deadline with my investigators so that we can have a timely turnaround for the client.

The next item that I include in the packet is a DVD or CD of captured activity and an overview of the investigation, using video and audio files. The audio and video files are taken from your hand held video cameras, digital cameras, DVR and voice recorders. I am assuming that you know how to get this data from your equipment to a computer, and then to a disk. If you do not know how to do that, recruit the help of somebody that knows the procedure. The least you can do is set up a time to visit the client to go over the activity that you have uncovered. If disks could not be burned, bring the actual electronic files with you so that the client can review it all with you. Have a printed report for the client, regardless of how you are to review the video and audio files.

Another item to add to the packet is your team's business card. I would suggest that you add four or five business cards for your client to hand out to family or friends. This will help stir up some future referrals. I love passing out my card. I have gotten a lot of referrals from pleased clients that know that we gave them our best. They know that I did everything in my power to assist them when they had nowhere to turn. Look, there are a lot of "groups" out there playing ghost hunter, and there are some that seem to have a plan together that will assure them some level of success. I get quality referrals because of my professionalism. Not just mine, but that of the individuals that accompany me to the investigation. I hand my card out because I know we can get the job done and because I am proud of my investigators and the way we conduct our business.

The client not only gets a memorable night out of the deal, they get the validation they seek when dealing with a haunting. They want to know that others can feel what they have felt. This is a strong bonding element that solidifies a new friendship, providing that you followed all the steps of a proper investigation and did your job professionally, respectfully and without judgment. My investigators treat the client like a family member from the onset of an investigation. We understand that they are concerned with an issue going on in their home. We make the client feel comfortable and we do this by being professional through our actions, behaviors, and mannerisms. We reiterate our professionalism with the packet that contains our findings.

In this photo: *Tom is investigating a defunct embalming room..*

"...*discover it, review it, and then understand it*".

Below deck of the U.S.S. Salem, Tom and Julie review some photos as two guests look on.
Photo by: Lisa Gurley (2010)

"My investigators treat the client like a family member"

Old graveyards are a great location to practice your sitting and listening skills.
In this photo: Toms' 1978 Land Rover Series 3 in a New Hampshire cemetery.

"You need to watch and listen with diligence".

PARATOM.COM

RIVERVIEW CEMETERY

GHOST WALK

NOVEMBER 20, 2010

Tom Lynch

PARATOM
INVESTIGATIVE UNIT

GROVELAND, MASSACHUSETTS

Join Tom Lynch and his **ParaTom Investigative Unit** for an evening of chills as they walk you into the unknown within the gates of the Historic Riverview Cemetery at Groveland, Massachusetts. 6:00 PM
Experience a live "EVP" and "Franks Box" session in the hopes of raising the voices of those departed. Arrive early and walk amongst the fascinating headstones of this historic site. Comfortable walking shoes and appropriate outerwear is recommended. Bring your flash cameras and flashlights as you never know what may show up!

Proceeds from this event will go towards the *Perpetual Care Fund* of this historic site. tickets can be purchased for $10.00 at WWW.PARATOM.COM or by contacting us at juliewilliams@paratom.com
We are limiting this exciting event to 25 guests. Buy your tickets early!

A poster from a SOLD OUT ParaTom event in November of 2010

Section Eleven
MEDIUMS ON A PARANORMAL INVESTIGATION

Julie Williams

What is the difference between a medium and a psychic? In short, a medium's job or task is to prove the continuity of life. A psychic predicts the future.

During a reading a medium will bring through a spirit and describe that person to you. They will tell you things that only you can recognize or make sense of. Understand this is not coming directly from the medium, but through the medium. Spirit is impressing upon or telling the medium what information to relay to you. You may not understand or recognize who or what is being brought through at the moment of the reading, but listen carefully and take it with you. Talk to other relatives and you may be surprised!

I experienced a perfect example of this on more than one occasion. I had a reading describing a man that passed with colon cancer, loved to sing and had a sense of humor. I could not place him but took the information with me. After discussing with my mom we realized it was my mom's cousin that had passed many years earlier! At another reading, a woman was described to me who I thought might be my great grandmother, although the clothing didn't sound quite right. I took it with me. While going through some old photos a few weeks later I found one of a woman dressed in the exact details the medium had mentioned. It was my great grandmother! I now have a photo of both relatives and several others in frames around my home. I didn't know them in life, but they visit and comfort me and try to guide me.

Many times, one will seek a reading from a medium and expect to hear from someone in particular that has passed and will either be disappointed that they didn't hear from that spirit or will think that the medium is a fake. Therefore, they won't listen to the information given to them. Having an open mind is very important. The one you wish to hear from won't necessarily be available to come through to you or may not have a message for you at that time.

Keep in mind that personalities don't change because one has passed on. If one was very quiet here and not talkative, you can't expect anything but when they cross over. If the person was a practical joker here on the Earth plane, they will probably continue to do so from the other side. The purpose of our physical life here is to learn lessons and to grow from them. You've heard of a wise soul or an old soul, even if the person is young. That term comes from the idea that a particular person has had many lives here on Earth and has learned many lessons, thus making the soul itself, very wise.

Julie on the set of 'Spektral Evidence" before her interview.

While on the other side, the soul continues to learn. Souls also tend to travel in soul groups, meaning your family now has probably shared multiple lives with you in the past but in a different role. For instance your parents today could have been your siblings, your children or grandparents in a previous life; they could have been a spouse a cousin or a distant relative.

Babies and children are still very closely connected to the spirit world when they arrive here. In some instances young children or toddlers will actually have memories of a prior life and be able to talk about them. You may also hear a toddler or young child talking to someone and we assume it is an "imaginary" friend. Many times it is a spirit that they are seeing. Because they are still closely connected to the spirit world, having just come from there, children often will see and communicate with spirit on a regular basis. When a child reaches the age of seven or eight, the logical mind has begun to form and take over and the adults in the child's life have begun to say "there is no such thing as ghosts". At that time, it is very common for sensitive children to lose their gift, or at least subdue it because society has taught them that it is wrong to see what they have been seeing.

Many times just before someone dies they will discuss seeing or dreaming of relatives that have passed before them. That is usually the spirit of those passed coming to greet the spirit of the one that is about to die. We never die alone, and we never cross over alone.

I am often asked the difference between a ghost and a spirit. Some will say a "ghost" is an earthbound spirit, one that has unfinished business or doesn't know they are dead, as is the case with a tragic passing. A spirit is one that has passed on and crossed over. They "check in" from time to time to bring love and comfort to those that are still here or to warn of danger. They try to guide us in the right direction for our soul's path. In my opinion, they are all spirits. Call it political correctness, but respect is the bottom line.

Now that you understand a bit about mediums and how they work and spirituality, you can follow along to see how I work on an investigation. I leave the scientific/technical part to Tom and I deal with the communication with the spirit.

As a medium on a paranormal investigation I have several responsibilities. Any investigation is exciting, the anticipation of actually contacting the other side and hopefully getting evidence is thrilling; however, I never go into an investigation without some kind of protection. Spiritual and/or psychic protection is what I am referring to. Obviously I don't go into an investigation to do readings, but I am potentially working with spirit in a very similar manner. I am trying to make contact and get answers, information from the spirit that I can later research to see if any of it can be validated.

There are two types of protection I practice. One of course, is prayer. I ask my God, guides and my angels to protect me and help me. I ask that they keep all of us safe and allow only those from the light, from the highest and best to be able to communicate with me. By practicing protection, I protect myself and the team from low-end spirits that may have the intent to harm, either spiritually or mentally. I also imagine a white light of protection surrounding me, our vehicle, and fellow investigators.

Aside from prayer, I carry my crystals with me. There are many crystals, raw and tumbled. They work in a variety of ways, from spiritual to physical. They are used in healing work as well as in meditation and mediumship. They protect against psychic attacks and negative energies from the living and the dead. I always wear my amethyst and carry my clear quartz. On investigations I also carry hematite, tiger's eye and a variety of others. What I choose to use on a particular investigation depends on the night, the location and my instincts. Sometimes my pockets are so full I think it adds five pounds!

There are many types of protection and it is a matter of personal choice. What works for one may not work for another. It is just important to practice some form. No one wants to bring a spirit home with them.

True Story:

Tom was followed home one time. He was at the home of a friend who had just returned from a paranormal event in Salem, Massachusetts. They were watching T.V. when all of a sudden; they heard a loud pop and crackling, as though somebody was balling up an empty bag of chips. Tom and his friend got up to investigate the source of the noise. They found nothing, at which time, it was about midnight and Tom called it a night and headed home. Home was 30 miles away.

As Tom was driving home, there was a sense of foreboding restlessness in the vehicle. When he arrived home at about 12:30A.M., Tom headed right up to bed. As he lay in bed, Tom felt that the room got a bit darker and restless. There was black swirling at the already dark ceiling and Tom was aware of this energy. It was not a good feeling.

As he tried to fall asleep, Tom heard that pop and crackling sound that he heard earlier at his friends' house. His head whipped to the left as a result of the loud noise, just in time to see what appeared to be blue electricity climbing the mini blinds in the bedroom. As the web-like blue light hit the metal curtain rod, it popped and dissipated. As it dissipated, the room seemed to lighten up and calm down.

The next morning, Tom called and asked his medium friend what he had done when he left the house and the mediums reply was "I cleansed the house of course". Tom laughed and said

"The entity left your house and caught up with me and followed me home". Tom theorizes that the entity attached itself to him and hung out for a while then dissipated and went back to Salem.

I also mentally make it known that no one is allowed to come home with me, both when we arrive on location and once we get into the vehicle to drive home. Anyone that was at the location when we arrived is to stay there or move on, but not follow us home or attach to us. Some people will circle their vehicle with a sprinkling of sea salt around the vehicle. Theoretically, spirits cannot cross over a line of sea salt. Some use holy water sprinkled on their vehicles or used to make the sign of the cross on their vehicles and even their equipment.

There are herbs that can be used as protection also, but those are used more for protection in your home, not necessarily to carry with you. Some herbs that can be used for clearing negative energies are aloe, barley, basil, bay leaf, cactus, carnation, cedar, chamomile, cinnamon, clove, cumin, curry, dill, eucalyptus, fennel, frankincense, garlic, ginseng, lavender, parsley, pepper, peppermint, rosemary, sage, thyme, violet. These are usually used by being placed in a bowl and left around the house.

When you buy crystals, you want to pick the one out of the bunch that "speaks" to you, the one that your eye is drawn to. You should pick up several, and see which one feels right, it will vibrate or you will feel your hand pulsate a bit if it is the right stone. A little meditation helps this. You may go to the store with the intent to purchase a particular crystal and walk out of the store with a different one. Let your intuition make the decision for you, spirit is letting you know there is a reason for it!

Cleansing and charging your stones, removes unwanted or negative energy from your crystals. There are several ways to do this. I usually use a salt water bath. (Although there are a few crystals that are sensitive to salt) I use sea salt and spring water or distilled water in a clear glass bowl. I start by lighting a white unscented candle that I place next to the bowl. I then say a short prayer, asking that all negative energies be removed from the stones and that they be cleansed and energized. I then soak the stones in the salt water for an hour or two, repeating my prayer and making my intentions known. Once I take the stones/crystals out of the water I lay them on a white cloth or white paper towel to dry.

After cleansing the stones, you need to program them, make them your own. You want to instill your intentions and your own energy into them. The easiest way to do this is to carry them in your pockets for seven days and sleep with them under your pillow. Once they are cleaned and charged/programmed never let anyone touch your stones. They are your own, you don't want other's energy on them or you'll have to clean them again.

Once a month I place my stones in the moonlight of the full moon to charge them. Once again I place them on a white cloth on the window sill for three consecutive nights when the moon is full. This charges and energizes them. (This can also be done to charge sea salt for future investigations by placing it in a bowl and then on the window sill) Even if it is a cloudy night, the moon will still charge the stones.

Your stones/crystals can also be cleansed by smudging. I use a white sage wand, which is used with an abalone shell. I always light a white unscented candle first, saying a prayer and making my intention known and then lighting the sage wand with the flame from the candle. You want to hold the crystals in the smoke of the sage while asking that all negative and unwanted energies be removed from the stones (also done to cleanse the house).

Protection complete, it is time to move on to the investigation. Another one of my responsibilities is to help locate the spirits, or possible spirits. I use my gifts to see, (clairvoyance) sense, (clairsentience) or feel what may be in the home. I can sometimes even hear (clairaudient) spirit. As an empath, (one that picks up on the emotions of the spirit) I sometimes will get physical symptoms that the spirit experienced in life before they passed. For me, not all my senses or gifts work at the same time. I think a lot depends on the location the particular spirit I am working with and whether or not I had proper time for meditation.

Proper equipment placement is necessary if you want to catch evidence. By tuning into any spirit or energy that may be in the building, I point out locations where I feel cameras or EVP work will be most successful. This discussion is all part of our pre-investigation team meeting on the way to the location. I will usually do a quick walkthrough with the other team members to get them acclimated to the building without discussion the case. I also use this walkthrough to reconnect and be sure I still feel the energy in the same areas as I did during the interview. There are times when the best laid plan is changed at the last minute.

During the investigation I will mention when I feel I am getting an impression or when I can sense or feel the energy change, which is usually a good indicator that we may have a better chance of capturing something on camera or video. Tom and I have worked together enough now that we can read each other very easily and he will know when I am picking something up and when to start taking photos.

Sometimes our equipment will start to pick something up and at that time I will tune in to try to get more information from the spirit to find out who is there and what they want. During an EVP session and I will try to communicate with the spirit and get information which helps us follow the correct line of questioning. It's a lot easier if they talk to me instead of having to wait to review the hours of audio we collect, but we do like to have the hard proof of the audio.

I also get the sense of when to quit. Sometimes as the night goes on, the lights on equipment stop blinking or slow down but the investigators keep going. Not only could that be an indication of spirit getting tired, but sometimes it is an indication that they are irritated. The last thing we want to do is disrespect the living or the dead and overstay our welcome. It doesn't do anyone any good. I can usually get a sense of when they leave the room or if they are agitated. At that point I ask that we bring the investigation to a close and we always thank the spirits for working with us. I offer an apology if I feel we have caused any distress to the spirit. In the end, it is the homeowner that has to live with this entity and we don't want them to have any negative backlash as the result of an agitated spirit.

By the end of the night, I guess one could say my job on a paranormal investigation, is to validate anything that the equipment may or may not have picked up and, in turn, the equipment hopefully validates anything that I may pick up. There are many groups out there that won't use mediums or psychics because they feel that a psychic or medium cannot be validated or proven. Actually, I often do research after the investigation for my own personal validation. I need to know if anything I picked up is accurate or makes sense. It is great when the homeowner knows the history involved and can validate on the spot, but many times all they can give us in their own personal accounts of any activity or experiences they have witnessed which may be similar to what I experience. Mediums are an important tool in a paranormal investigators tool kit.

"I often do research after the investigation for my own personal validation."

A sage wand and an abalone shell, crystals and medallions are a source of protection.

Julie goes over a client report at a psychic fair in Salem, NH

Section Twelve

MEET THE INVESTIGATIVE UNIT

Though I am a freelance investigator, I could not do my clients justice without the few individuals that I have chosen to work with me. Handpicked for their unique talents, each brings with them, to an investigation, dedication, attention and compassion to the client. I am proud to call the following individuals, my team.

**Phil Lynch
videographer- Investigator**

"I have been with ParaTom for an eventful year and a half. I am blessed to be a part of the ParaTom Investigative Unit and to be under the guidance and training of my Uncle Tom.

When I was young, I was playing in my room. I decided to go to my closet to get more toys. As I opened my closet door expecting to see my toy chest I found a different surprise, and believe me, it sure wasn't a nice one. Standing before me was an elderly woman with white hair just staring at me. When I told my parents, they thought it was my imagination. Until that Christmas at my grandmothers' house, that is. My grandmother called me over to her lap and showed me a picture with three women. She asked me if any of these women were in my closet. When I pointed to the woman that I had seen, she told me that that woman was my great grandmother and that she died while owning the house that I live in. It was that night that my parents and I knew there was something paranormal afoot.

So far, my two favorite investigations with the ParaTom Investigative Unit have been a Funeral Home where I had seen a little boy peeking around the corner at me, from the top of a set of stairs. Secondly, private investigations in Marlboro, Massachusetts, where I had heard footsteps on the floor directly above me and also saw mist appear in front of our thermal cameras."

Phil listens as Tom recaps the evening's events in Marlboro, Massachusetts (2010)

"Standing before me was an elderly woman with white hair just staring at me."

Lori Gath Hand
Medium- Investigator

"I started to realize in my teens that I had the ability to "feel" things that my friends and family could not. At times I was able to sense the presence of spirit and emotion when entering an area. In my later teens, I started to get visions of things and predictions of events like date of delivery and sex of baby for pregnant couples. In an effort to educate myself on these abilities and to develop my skill, I started talking with psychics, mediums, and other people that I knew with the abilities. Eventually, I found my way to Julie Williams, and a friendship forged. Julie introduced me to a

spiritualist church and there, I have been learning to work with and grow my skills and have also been working with Tom Lynch and the ParaTom Investigative Unit, joining them on investigations and public events. I enjoy working with Tom Lynch and all aspects of spiritualism and working with spirit."

Lori Hand is running video cable to the second floor before an investigation.

"At times I was able to sense the presence of spirit"

Julie Williams
Manager-Medium-Investigator

"I was aware of "ghosts" at a very early age. I can remember talking to my mom about them since childhood. She always referred to us a "sensitives". She would tell me stories of her grandmother and aunt taking her to the spiritualist church on occasion as a child. She would always get readings.

Through my teenage years I had dreams that would come true and I had such a gut feeling for things, I knew I couldn't get away with not trusting my inner thoughts. One such experience sticks out in my mind. At a time when seatbelts were not mandatory I stopped half way out of the driveway one morning to put it on. I had never worn it before. Almost at my destination I had an accident and the seatbelt saved me from going through the windshield! I'd say that was a perfect example of how spirit works with us. As I got older I noticed that I seemed to have more and more experiences with the unknown and I could no longer ignore it or quite explain it. We also discovered that my daughter had begun to develop her own gifts that she needed to understand. I set out to find some answers to our many, many questions.

After getting my feet wet with public event/fundraiser types of ghost hunts, I contacted Tom and asked to attend a "real" investigation. I knew there was more of a scientific approach to investigations. I wanted to see firsthand what went on without all the fan fair. I wanted a chance to try my gifts on my own, without distractions from large groups of people. I am thankful to Tom for allowing me to join him that night. I continue to learn from Tom, and I have found that spiritualist church and attend regularly. I also attend weekly classes at the church and continue to hone my abilities."

In this photo: Julie is posing near a memorial in Bradford Burial Ground

Julie and Tom in a Bradford, Massachusetts cemetery, for some photo gathering.

"I was aware of "ghosts" at a very early age."

Deb O'Leary
Guest Medium-Investigator
Pelham Paranormal Research

"It never occurred to me that not everyone can see, hear and sense spirits. I thought it was part of being human, that is until I married my husband, Joe. When I told him about the "spirit thing", I think he was placating me. "Sure Honey, whatever you say" kind of stuff. I was just happy to have someone not think I was crazy! Until one night, about 2 years into our marriage, Joe believed. Joe is a night owl and I turn in early. I was sound asleep only to be woken up to Joe, pounding on my leg! There was a man spirit, standing at the end of our bed!

Deb O'Leary of Pelham Paranormal Research on an investigation in Haverhill, MA

I was annoyed to be woken up, but he (Joe) was petrified! That's when I think Joe REALLY believed that spirits sought me out.

I let him know that I also like to do paranormal investigating. If that's what I needed to stay sane while raising 2 girls, 14 months apart, go ahead! So I did. I began Pelham Paranormal Research. We are a small group of investigators who like to rely on our psychic abilities.

We have investigated many places including the Lizzie Borden House and the U.S.S. Hornet, to name a few. Although things were going well, it was time to branch out. That's when I met Tom Lynch and Julie Williams of Paratom. I was thrilled to be asked to join them on a private home investigation! What an amazing experience! Tom and Julie did the initial interview of that home. When they determined that things were legitimate in that house, we did the investigation. This house was perhaps the most "haunted" and captivating investigation that I have ever been on! There were noises and smells in that house. There were personal experiences and apparitions. These were things that I will never forget. I look forward to more investigations with the Paratom Investigative Unit."

"It never occurred to me that not everyone can see, hear and sense spirits."

Photo
Album

Suggestion

Tom with the ParaTom information table at a psychic fair. Putting these types of information tables at events like this helps get your name and services out there. Because of this one event, Tom was given television and radio interviews, plus a few quality investigations. Google "psychic fairs" and see what comes up!

Approaching Buffalo Central Terminal in Buffalo, New York (2009)

This stairway that once echoed with the sounds of employees at Buffalo Central Terminal, now lays abandoned and littered with the old papers of a once thriving hub.

Coffee in hand, Tom points to a few ParaTom event flyers that were hung in the window of a local business in Salem, New Hampshire. (2010)

NOTE:
Table tipping is a form of spirit communication. That awesome t-shirt is a form of advertising!

Staff mediums, Lori and Julie, demonstrate "table tipping". A form of spirit communication.

Go online and learn more about table tipping.

Tom is getting ready to depart the site of a very active residence in Windham, New Hampshire

Julie stands at an old grave site in Salem, New Hampshire.

Julie between decks of the U.S.S. Salem during the investigation of this awesome ship.

A rare site indeed. A new grave in an old section of the Riverview Cemetery in Groveland, MA.

The empty graves of our nations veterans. It was a wonder to see the absolute uniformity of these precision dug graves at the National Veterans Cemetery in Saratoga, New York.

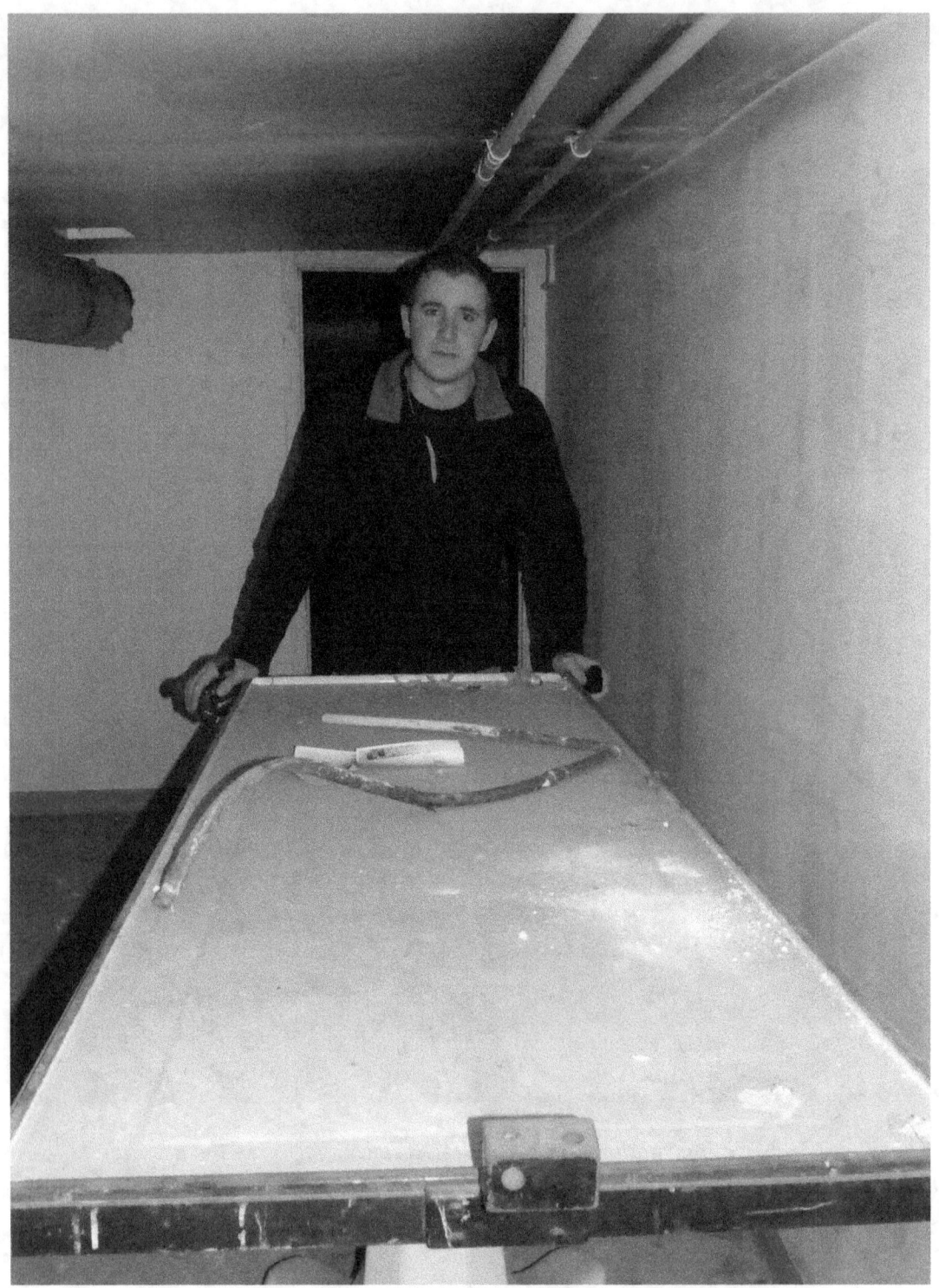

Phil in the embalming room of an old Funeral Home (2009)

The basement stairway of an old funeral home that leads to the embalming room.

Julie's son, Evan, in the Fort Constitution powder magazine. Portsmouth, New Hampshire.

www.ParaTom.com
Proud sponsor of

*A postcard that Tom used during the period that ParaTom.com was a sponsor of Para-X Radio, which can still be heard at **www.para-x.com*** *(2009)*

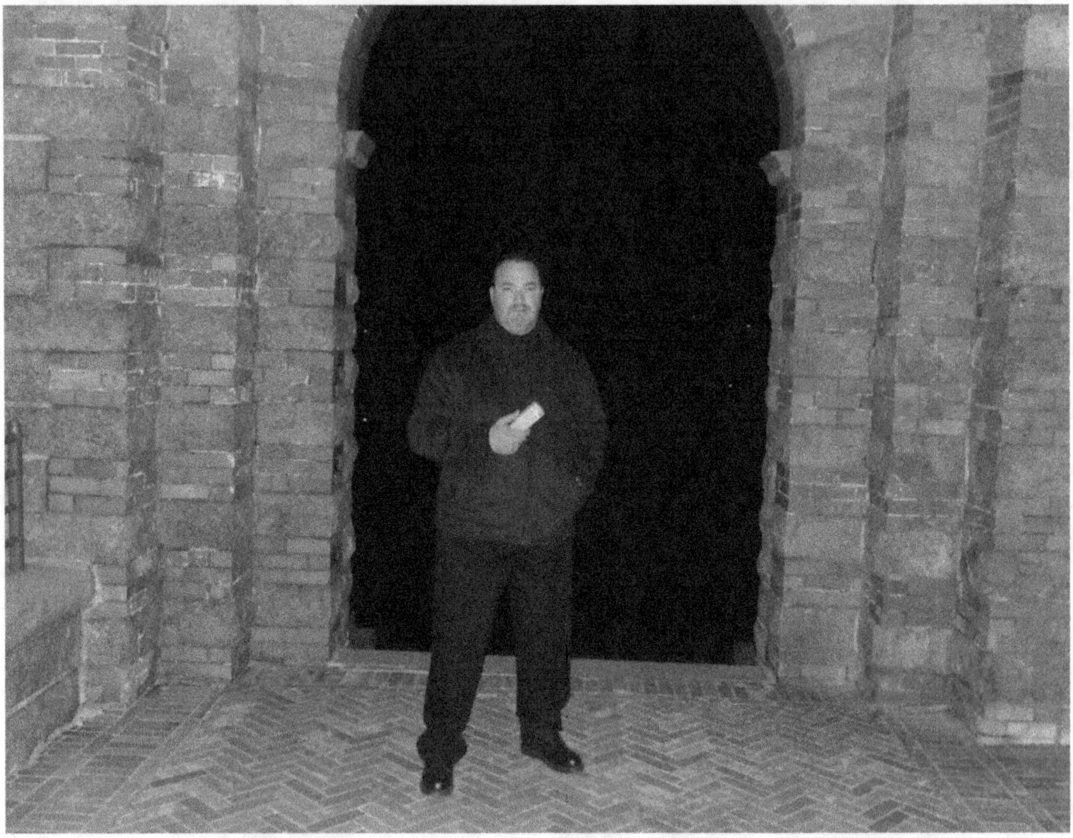

Tom at the remains of the historic Tenney Castle in Methuen, Massachusetts. (2008)

The ParaTom Investigative Unit Logo

V.I.P. parking outside of Buffalo Central Terminal, Buffalo, New York (2009)

*A big thanks to **Western New York Ghost Hunters** for having me out for the visit.*

Buffalo Central Terminal was such an amazingly large building, we couldn't see it all! It must have been a sight to see in its day! In the 1940's, Men shipped out to war here and never returned.

Tom with friend and author, Beth Brown, at a Fort Mifflin event in Philadelphia. (2009)

Riverview Cemetery, Groveland , Massachusetts has some of the oldest graves in the area. Ghost stories abound in this old cemetery.

Long exposures can capture the red "focus" light of another camera to create effects.

Tom with friend and author, Lori McCabe in the library of the haunted Hawthorne Hotel, in Salem, Massachusetts.

Lighthouses along the New England coast have had their share of ghost stories over the years

"Go online to learn more about this haunted lighthouses."

Tom finds and points to a ParaTom postcard hanging in Salem, Massachusetts

Julie and daughter, Tori, receiving their membership at a spiritual church.

Tom with an early New England gravestone.

NOTE Pad

NOTES:

NOTES:

NOTES:

NOTES:

If you would like to contact the
ParaTom Investigative Unit
Please free to email us at:

tomlynch@paratom.com

juliewilliams@paratom.com

VISIT US AT:

www.PARATOM.com

and

✓ Sign the guestbook

✓ Report a haunting

✓ Learn more about us

✓ Follow us on Facebook

Tom heads to Gardner, Massachusetts for the investigation of the year!
Be one of ten guest investigators to join Tom and his Investigative Unit
to help unravel the mysteries of this old Victorian home.

Tickets now on sale at www.ParaTom.com